ARUBA CERTIFIED CLEARPASS PROFESSIONAL – ACCP (HPE6-A68) EXAM PRACTICE QUESTIONS & DUMPS

EXAM STUDY GUIDE FOR ACCP
(HPE6-A68) Exam Prep LATEST VERSION

Presented By: Quantic Books

About Quantic Books:

Quantic Books is a publishing house based in Princeton, New Jersey, USA. , a platform that is accessible online as well as locally, which gives power to educational content, erudite collection, poetry & many other book genres. We make it easy for writers & authors to get their books designed, published, promoted, and sell professionally on worldwide scale with eBook + Print distribution. Quantic Books is now distributing books worldwide.

Note: Find answers of the questions at the last of the book.

QUESTION 1

Refer to the screenshot below:

View Endpoint

MAC Address	98b8e362fddf	IP Address	192.168.1.252
Description		Static IP	FALSE
Status	Unknown	Hostname	
Added by	Policy Manager	MAC Vendor	Apple
		Category	SmartDevice
		OS Family	Apple
		Device Name	Apple iPad
		Updated At	Apr 10, 2013 19:47:28 UTC
		Show Fingerprint	☑

Endpoint Fingerprint Details

Host User Agent	Mozilla/5.0 (iPad; CPU OS 6_0_2 like Mac OS X) AppleWebKit/536.26 (KHTML, like Gecko) Version/6.0 Mobile/10A8500 Safari/8536.25
DHCP Option55	["1,3,6,15,119,252"]
DHCP Options	["53,55,57,61,50,51,12"]

Based upon Endpoint information presented here, which collectors were used to profile the device as Apple iPad? (Select 2)

A. OnGuard Agent
B. HTTP User-Agent
C. DHCP fingerprinting
D. SNMP
E. SmartDevice

QUESTION 2

To setup an Aruba Controller as DHCP relay for device fingerprinting, which of the given IP addresses needs to be organized?

A. DHCP server IP
B. ClearPass server IP
C. Active Directory IP
D. Microsoft NPS server IP
E. Switch IP

QUESTION 3

What database in the Policy Manager comprises the device features derived by profiling?

A. Local Users Repository
B. Onboard Devices Repository
C. Endpoints Repository
D. Guest User Repository
E. User Repository

QUESTION 4

Refer to the screenshot below:

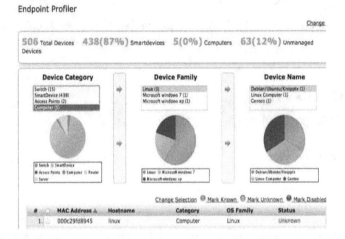

Endpoint Profiler

Change

506 Total Devices   438(87%) Smartdevices   5(0%) Computers   63(12%) Unmanaged Devices

Device Category	Device Family	Device Name
Switch (15)	Linux (3)	Debian/Ubuntu/Knoppix (1)
SmartDevice (438)	Microsoft windows 7 (1)	Linux Computer (1)
Access Points (2)	Microsoft windows xp (1)	Centoo (1)
Computer (5)		

#	MAC Address ▲	Hostname	Category	OS Family	Status
1.	000c29fd8945	linux	Computer	Linux	Unknown

Change Selection ⊖ Mark Known ⊖ Mark Unknown ● Mark Disabled

Based on the Endpoint Profiler output presented here, which of the given statements is accurate?

A. The devices have been profiled using DHCP fingerprinting.
B. There are 5 devices profiled in the Computer Device Group.
C. Apple devices will be profiled in the SmartDevice group.
D. There is just only 1 Microsoft Windows device present in the network.
E. The linux device with MAC address 000c29fd8945 has not been profiled.

QUESTION 5

Which of the given conditions can be used for rule creation of an Enforcement Policy? (Select 3)

A. System Time
B. Clearpass IP address
C. Posture
D. Switch VLAN
E. Connection Protocol

QUESTION 6

Refer to the screenshot below:

Based on the Enforcement Policy configuration, if a user with Role Engineer connects to the network and the posture token allotted is Unidentified, what Enforcement Profile will be operated?

A. WORKER_VLAN
B. Remote Worker ACL
C. RestrictedACL
D. Deny Access Profile
E. HR VLA

QUESTION 7

Which of the given components of a Policy Service is compulsory?

A. Enforcement
B. Posture
C. Profiler
D. Role Mapping Policy
E. Authorization Source

QUESTION 8

Which of the given options is the correct order of steps of a Policy Service request?

1) Clearpass tests the request against Service Rules to select a Policy Service.
2) Clearpass applies the Enforcement Policy.
3) Negotiation of the Verification Method happens among the NAD and Clearpass.
4) Clearpass sends the Enforcement Profile features to the NAD.
5) NAD forwards verification request to Clearpass.

A. 1, 3, 2, 4, 5
B. 5, 1, 3, 2, 4
C. 5, 1, 3, 4, 2
D. 1, 2, 3, 4, 5
E. 2, 3, 4, 5, 1

QUESTION 9

Which of the given information is NOT needed while building a Policy Service for 802.1X verification?

A. Network Access Device used
B. Verification Method used
C. Verification Source used
D. Posture Token of the user
E. Profiling information of the user

QUESTION 10

Which of the given components can use Active Directory authorization features for the decision-making process? (Select 2)

A. Role Mapping Policy
B. Posture Policy
C. Enforcement Policy
D. Service Rules

QUESTION 11

What information can we conclude from the given graph?

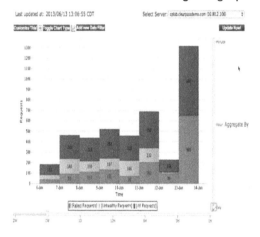

A. This graph identifies all verification requests got by Clearpass in one year.
B. This graph identifies all verification requests got by Clearpass in a day.
C. The graph identifies all verification requests got by Clearpass in a month.
D. Each bar identifies total verification requests per minute.
E. Each bar identifies total verification requests per day.

QUESTION 12

What information can we conclude from the above audit row detail?
(Select 2)

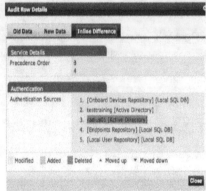

A. radius01 was added as an verification source.

B. radius01 was deleted from the list of verification sources.

C. The policy service was moved to position number 3.

D. The policy service was moved to position number 4.

E. radius01 was moved to position number 4.

QUESTION 13

What is the aim of the Audit Viewer in the Monitoring section of
ClearPass Policy Manager?

A. To audit user verifications.

B. To audit the network for PCI compliance.

C. To display the entire configuration of the ClearPass Policy Manager.

D. To display changes made to the ClearPass configuration.

E. To display system events.

QUESTION 14

If the "Alerts" tab in an verification session details tab in Access Tracker displays the given error message "Access denied by policy", what could be a probable reason for verification failure?

A. Execution of an Enforcement Policy
B. Execution of a firewall policy
C. Failure to categorize the request in a Clearpass service
D. Execution of a Posture Policy
E. Failure to activate the enforcement policy

QUESTION 15

If a user's verification is failing and there are no entries in the Clearpass's Access Tracker, which of the given is a probable reason for the verification failure?

A. The user used a wrong password.
B. The user is not found in the database.
C. The shared secret among Network Access Device and Clearpass does not match.
D. The user account has expired.
E. The user's certificate is invalid.

QUESTION 16

Which of the given statements is accurate based on the Access
Tracker output presented below?

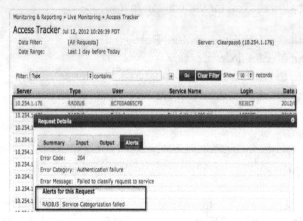

A. The user wireless profile is incorrectly setup.
B. Clearpass does not have a service allowed for MAC verification.
C. The user MAC address is not present in the Endpoints table in the
   Clearpass database.
D. The user used incorrect credentials to verify to the network.
E. The RADIUS user on the Windows server failed to categorize the
   service correctly.

QUESTION 17

What kinds of files are stored in the Local Shared Folders database in
Clearpass? (Select 2)

A. Backup Files
B. Software image
C. Log files
D. Generated Reports
E. Device fingerprint dictionaries

QUESTION 18

A University wants to deploy ClearPass with the Guest module. They have two kinds of users that need to use web login verification. The first kind of users are students whose accounts are in their Active Directory Server. The second kind of users are friends of students who need to self-register to access the network.

How must the service be setup in the Policy Manager for this Network?

A. Make a service with the Guest User Repository as the Verification Source and the Active Directory Server as the authorization source.
B. Make a service with the Active Directory Server as the Verification Source and the Guest User Repository as the authorization source.
C. Make a service with the Guest User Repository and Active Directory servers as Verification Sources.
D. Make a service with just only the Guest user Repository as the verification source, and Guest User Repository and Active Directory server as authorization sources.
E. Make a service with the Guest User Repository or Active Directory server as the single Verification Source.

QUESTION 19

Which of the given use cases will need a ClearPass Guest application license? (Select 2)

A. Sponsor based guest user access
B. Worker personal device registration
C. User self-registration for access
D. Guest device fingerprinting
E. Endpoint health assessment

QUESTION 20

Below is a screenshot of the Guest Role Mapping Policy:

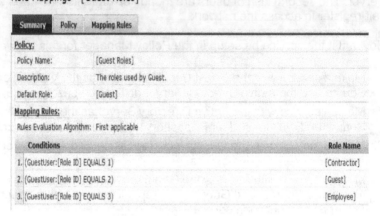

What is the aim of this Role Mapping Policy?

A. To send a firewall role back to the controller based on the Guest User's Role ID.
B. To allot Controller roles to guests.
C. To display a role name on the Self-registration receipt page.
D. To allot ClearPass roles to guests based on the guest's Role ID as seen for the duration of verification.
E. To allot all 3 roles of [Contractor], [Guest] and [Worker] to every guest user.

QUESTION 21

An administrator logs in to the Guest module in ClearPass and under 'List Accounts' sees the given:

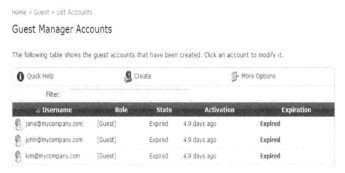

Guest Manager Accounts

The following table shows the guest accounts that have been created. Click an account to modify it.

	Quick Help		Create		More Options

Filter:

△ Username	Role	State	Activation	Expiration
jane@mycompany.com	[Guest]	Expired	4.9 days ago	Expired
john@mycompany.com	[Guest]	Expired	4.9 days ago	Expired
kim@mycompany.com	[Guest]	Expired	4.9 days ago	Expired

If a user with username kim@mycompany.com tries to access the Web Login page, what would we expect to happen?

A. The user will not be able to access the Web Login page.

B. The user will be able to login and verify effectively but they will be instant disconnected after.

C. The user will not be able to login and verify.

D. The user will be able to login for the next 4.9 days, but after this they will not be able to login anymore.

QUESTION 22

Refer to the screenshot below:

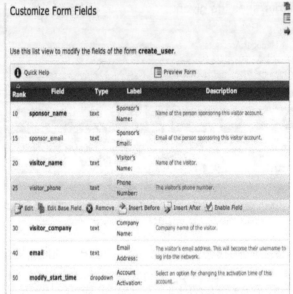

Customize Form Fields

Use this list view to modify the fields of the form **create_user**.

Rank	Field	Type	Label	Description
10	**sponsor_name**	text	Sponsor's Name:	Name of the person sponsoring this visitor account.
15	sponsor_email	text	Sponsor's Email:	Email of the person sponsoring this visitor account.
20	**visitor_name**	text	Visitor's Name:	Name of the visitor.
25	visitor_phone	text	Phone Number:	The visitor's phone number.
30	**visitor_company**	text	Company Name:	Company name of the visitor.
40	**email**	text	Email Address:	The visitor's email address. This will become their username to log into the network.
50	**modify_start_time**	dropdown	Account Activation:	Select an option for changing the activation time of this account.

Edit Edit Base Field Remove Insert Before Insert After Enable Field

Based on the above configuration, which of the given statements is accurate?

A. The visitor_phone field will be noticeable to operator making the account.
B. The visitor_phone field will be noticeable to the guest users in the web login page.
C. The visitor_company field will be noticeable to operator making the account.
D. The visitor_company field will be noticeable to the guest users in the web login page.
E. The email field will be noticeable to guest users on the web login page.

QUESTION 23

Refer to the screenshot below:

Based on the above configuration which of the given statements is accurate?

A. Just only guest users connecting to SSID Aruba will be permitted access to the network by ClearPass Guest.

B. The minimum password length for guest passwords is set to a default value of 8.

C. The usernames generated for guest users by Guest Manager will be a combination of random numbers.

D. The password generated for guest users by Guest Manager will be a combination of random numbers.

QUESTION 24

Refer to the screenshot in the exhibit below, as seen when configuring a Web Login Page in ClearPass Guest:

Home » Configuration » Web Logins

RADIUS Web Login

Use this form to make changes to the RADIUS Web Login **Guest Network**.

RADIUS Web Login Editor	
* Name:	Guest Network Enter a name for this web login page.
Page Name:	Aruba_login Enter a page name for this web login. The web login will be accessible from "/guest/page_name.php".
Description:	 Comments or descriptive text about the web login.
* Vendor Settings:	Aruba Networks ▾ Select a predefined group of settings suitable for standard network configurations.
Address:	securelogin.arubanetworks.com Enter the IP address or hostname of the vendor's product here.
Secure Login:	Use vendor default ▾ Select a security option to apply to the web login process.
Dynamic Address:	☐ The controller will send the IP to submit credentials In multi-controller deployments, it is often required to post credentials to different add The address above will be used whenever the parameter is not available or fails the re

What is the page name field used for?

A. For Administrators to access the PHP page, but not guests.
B. For Administrators to reference the page just only.
C. For forming the Web Login Page URL.
D. For forming the Web Login Page URL and the page name that guests needs to configure on their laptop wireless supplicant.
E. For forming the Web Login Page URL where Administrators add guest users.

QUESTION 25
Below is a screenshot of a user connecting to a Guest SSID:

Based on the image presented above, which of the given best defines the user's state?

A. The user verified through the web login page first before it was able to obtain an IP address.

B. The user does not have an IP address, but they have verified through the web login page.

C. The user does not have an IP address for the reason that they have not verified through the web login page yet.

D. We can't tell from the image above.

QUESTION 26

A Bank would like to deploy ClearPass Guest with web login verification so that their customers can self-register on the network to get network access when they have meetings with Bank Personnel. Still, they're worried about security.

Which of the given is accurate? (Select 3)

A. For the duration of web login verification, if HTTPS is used for the web login page, guest credentials will be encrypted.
B. If HTTPS is used for the web login page, after verification is completed guest Internet traffic will all be encrypted as well.
C. If HTTPS is used for the web login page, after verification is completed some guest Internet traffic may be unencrypted.
D. After verification, an IPSEC VPN on the guest's user can be used to encrypt Internet traffic.
E. HTTPS must never be used for Web Login Page verification.

QUESTION 27

A Hospital would like to deploy ClearPass Guest for friends and relatives of patients to access the Internet. They would like patients to be able to access an internal webpage on the intranet where they can view patient information. Still, other guests must not have access to this page.

Which of the given is accurate? (Select 2)

A. The NAD device will be firewalling users to block Intranet traffic.
B. ClearPass will be firewalling users to block Intranet traffic.
C. It's essential for us to have two separate web login pages because the different access necessities of patients and guests.
D. We will need to configure different Enforcement actions for patients and guests in the service.
E. Both the NAD and Clearpass would have to firewall users to block traffic.

QUESTION 28

Below is a screenshot of a self-registration receipt:

Which of the given is accurate?

A. Expiration time for guest accounts can be modified by the visitor.
B. Receipt Actions such as 'Download account details' cannot be modified in the self-registration editor.
C. Corporation Name field cannot be removed from the registration page using the self-registration editor.
D. The user will just only be able to login among the Activation and Expiration time.
E. The user needs to be logged in before they can use the 'Download account details' link.

QUESTION 29

A corporation deployed the guest Self-registration with Sponsor Approval workflow for their guest SSID. The administrator logs into the Policy Manager and sees the given in the Guest User Repository:

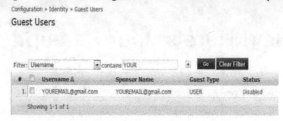

Configuration » Identity » Guest Users

Guest Users

Filter: Username [▾] contains YOUR [+] [Go] [Clear Filter]

#	Username ▲	Sponsor Name	Guest Type	Status
1.	YOUREMAIL@gmail.com	YOUREMAIL@gmail.com	USER	Disabled

Showing 1-1 of 1

What can you conclude from the above? (Select 2)

A. The guest has submitted the registration form.
B. The guest has not submitted the registration form yet.
C. The sponsor has confirmed the guest account.
D. The sponsor has not confirmed the guest account yet.
E. The user's account is active.

QUESTION 30

Refer to the screenshot below of a MAC Caching enforcement policy:

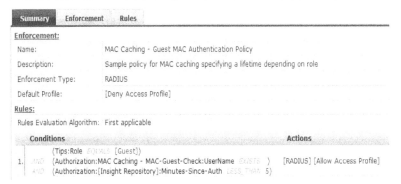

Configuration » Enforcement » Policies » Edit - MAC Caching - Guest MAC Authentication Policy

Enforcement Policies - MAC Caching - Guest MAC Authentication Policy

Summary	Enforcement	Rules

Enforcement:

Name:	MAC Caching - Guest MAC Authentication Policy
Description:	Sample policy for MAC caching specifying a lifetime depending on role
Enforcement Type:	RADIUS
Default Profile:	[Deny Access Profile]

Rules:

Rules Evaluation Algorithm: First applicable

Conditions	Actions
1. (Tips:Role EQUALS [Guest]) AND (Authorization:MAC Caching - MAC-Guest-Check:UserName EXISTS) AND (Authorization:[Insight Repository]:Minutes-Since-Auth LESS_THAN 5)	[RADIUS] [Allow Access Profile]

Which of the given is accurate?

A. Just only a user with Controller role of [Guest] will be permitted to verify

B. Just only a user with Clearpass role of [Guest] and that has verified using the web login page less than 5 minutes ago, will have their MAC verification succeed

C. Just only a user with Clearpass role of [Guest] and that has verified using the web login page more than 5 minutes ago, will have their MAC verification succeed

D. Just only a user whose last MAC verification was less than 5 minutes ago, will have their MAC verification succeed

QUESTION 31

Refer to the screenshot below

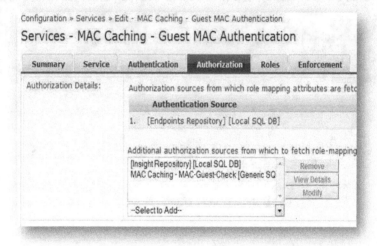

Configuration » Services » Edit - MAC Caching - Guest MAC Authentication

Services - MAC Caching - Guest MAC Authentication

| Summary | Service | Authentication | Authorization | Roles | Enforcement |

Authorization Details:

Authorization sources from which role mapping attributes are fetc

Authentication Source

1. [Endpoints Repository] [Local SQL DB]

Additional authorization sources from which to fetch role-mapping

[Insight Repository] [Local SQL DB]
MAC Caching - MAC-Guest-Check [Generic SQ

Remove
View Details
Modify

--Select to Add--

Which of the given is accurate of the MAC-Guest-Check SQL query authorization source?

A. It's used to check if the MAC address status is known in the endpoints table
B. It's used to check if the guest account has expired
C. It's used to check if the MAC address status is unidentified in the endpoints table
D. It's used to check how long it's been since the last web login verification
E. It's used to check if the MAC address is in the MAC Caching repository

QUESTION 32

Refer to the screenshot below:

Why is the Insight Repository used as an authorization source for this MAC verification service?

A. To check how long ago the last web login verification was done

B. To check how many sessions ago the last web login verification was done

C. To check how long ago the last MAC verification was done

D. To run a report when the user verifies

E. To validate the user's MAC address against the endpoints table

QUESTION 33

Below is a screenshot of a user's laptop:

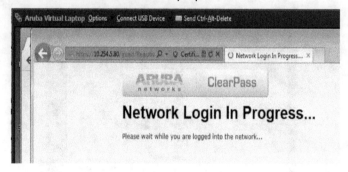

What would you expect to happen next?

A. The web login page will be displayed.
B. The user will be presented with a self-registration receipt.
C. The NAD device will send an verification request to ClearPass.
D. The user will send a NAS verification request to ClearPass.
E. Clearpass will send a NAS verification request to the NAD device.

QUESTION 34

Below is a screenshot of a user logged in to the Self-Service Portal:

Notice the traffic got and traffic sent statistics. Which of the given is accurate?

A. These show the total amount of traffic the guest transmitted after account expiration, as seen through RADIUS accounting messages sent from the NAD to ClearPass.
B. These show the total amount of traffic the guest transmitted, as seen through RADIUS accounting messages sent from the NAD to ClearPass.
C. These show the total amount of traffic the NAD transmitted to ClearPass, as seen through RADIUS accounting messages from the NAD to ClearPass.
D. These show the total amount of traffic the guest transmitted, as seen through RADIUS CoA packets from the NAD to ClearPass.

QUESTION 35

An administrator allowed the Pre-auth check for their guest self-registration. At what stage in the registration process is this check performed?

A. Before the user self-registers.
B. After the user self-registers; before the user logs in.
C. After the user logs in; before the NAD sends an verification request.
D. After the user logs in; after the NAD sends an verification request.
E. When a user is re-authenticating to the network.

QUESTION 36

A hotel chain in recent times deployed ClearPass Guest. A guest enters the hotel and connects to the Guest SSID. They launch their web browser and kind in www.google.com, but they're not able to instantly see the web login page.

Which of the given could be causing this? (Select 2):

A. The DNS server is not replying with an IP address for www.google.com.
B. The guest is using a Linux laptop which doesn't support web login.
C. The ClearPass server has a server certificate issued by Verisign.
D. The ClearPass server has a server certificate issued by the internal Microsoft Certificate Server.
E. The ClearPass server does not recognize the user's certificate.

QUESTION 37

Refer to the screenshot below of a MAC Caching service:

A guest connects to the Guest SSID and verifies effectively using the guest.php web login page. Which of the given is accurate?

A. Their MAC address will be noticeable in the Endpoints table with Known Status.
B. Their MAC address will be noticeable in the Endpoints table with Unidentified Status.
C. Their MAC address will be noticeable in the Guest User Repository with Known Status.
D. Their MAC address will be noticeable in the Guest User Repository with Unidentified Status.
E. Their MAC address will be deleted from the Endpoints table.

QUESTION 38

A corporation executed the Self-Registration with Sponsor Approval workflow for their Guest SSID. A guest connects to the Guest SSID, then self-registers. They see the given on their user device:

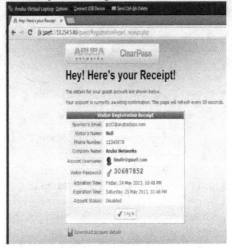

Which of the given is accurate?

A. The Sponsor approved the guest already.
B. The Sponsor has not approved the guest yet.
C. A confirmation email was sent to the sponsor at limdir@gmail.com.
D. A guest registration receipt was sent to p1t3@arubaclass.com.
E. The guest is ready to login using their username and password.

QUESTION 39

Refer to the screenshot below outlining a guest Self-Registration with Sponsor Approval workflow:

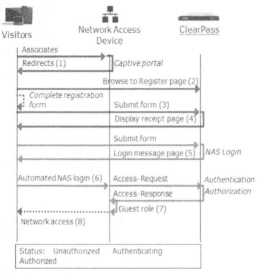

At which stage is an email request sent to the sponsor?

A. After 'Redirects (1)'
B. After 'Submit form (3)'
C. After 'Login Message page (5)'
D. After 'Automated NAS login (6)'
E. After 'Guest Role (7)'

QUESTION 40

What are these RADIUS features used for in the Aruba RADIUS dictionary presented here?

RADIUS Dictionaries

#	Attribute Name	ID	Type	In/Out
1.	Aruba-User-Role	1	String	in out
2.	Aruba-User-Vlan	2	Unsigned32	in out
3.	Aruba-Priv-Admin-User	3	Unsigned32	in out
4.	Aruba-Admin-Role	4	String	in out
5.	Aruba-Essid-Name	5	String	in out
6.	Aruba-Location-Id	6	String	in out
7.	Aruba-Port-Id	7	String	in out
8.	Aruba-Template-User	8	String	in out
9.	Aruba-Named-Vlan	9	String	in out
10.	Aruba-AP-Group	10	String	in out

Vendor Name: Aruba (14823)

A. To send information via RADIUS packets to users.
B. To send information via RADIUS packets to Aruba NADs.
C. To gather information about Aruba NADs for ClearPass.
D. To gather and send Aruba NAD information to ClearPass.
E. To send CoA packets from Clearpass to the Aruba NAD.

QUESTION 41

Define the aim of the Aruba TACACS+ dictionary as presented here:

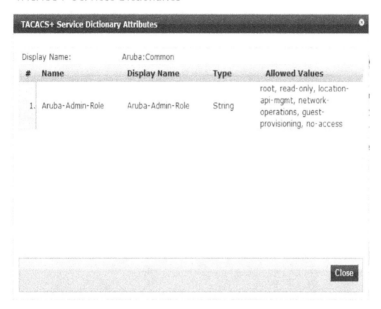

A. The Aruba-Admin-Role attribute is used to allot different privileges to users for the duration of 802.1X verification.
B. The Aruba-Admin-Role attribute is used by ClearPass to allot TIPS roles to users for the duration of 802.1X verification.
C. The Aruba-Admin-Role attribute is used to allot different privileges to administrators logging into an Aruba NAD device.
D. The Aruba-Admin-Role attribute is used to allot different privileges to administrators logging into ClearPass.
E. The Aruba-Admin-Role on the controller is operated to users using TACACS+ to login to the Policy Manager.

QUESTION 42

Refer to the screenshot in the exhibit below, which illustrates the configuration of a Windows 802.1X supplicant.

What will choosing 'Validate server certificate' do?

A. The user will send its certificate to the server for verification.
B. The server will send its private key to the user for verification.
C. The server and user will perform an HTTPS SSL certificate exchange.
D. The user will verify the server certificate against a trusted CA.
E. The user will send its private key to the server for verification.

QUESTION 43

Refer to the screenshot in the exhibit below, which illustrates the configuration of a Windows 802.1X supplicant.

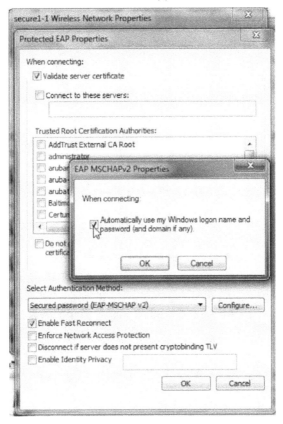

If 'Automatically use my Windows logon name and password' are selected, which of the given is accurate?

A. The user's Windows login username and password will be sent in a EAP frame to the Verification Server.

B. The user's Windows login username and password will be sent in a RADIUS Accounting frame to the Verification server.

C. The user will need to re-verify every time they connect to the network.

D. The user's Windows logon name and password will be sent via a TACACS+ frame to the verification server.

E. The user will prompt the user to enter the logon username and password.

QUESTION 44

What does a user need for it to perform EAP-PEAP effectively, if 'Validate Server Certificate' is not allowed?

A. Username and Password
B. User Certificate
C. Pre-shared key
D. Certificate Authority
E. Server Certificate

QUESTION 45

What is RADIUS CoA used for?

A. To verify users or devices before granting them access to a network.
B. To force the user to re-verify upon roaming to a new Controller.
C. To apply firewall policies based on verification credentials.
D. To validate a host MAC against a white and a black list.
E. To transmit messages to the NAD/NAS to modify a user's session status.

QUESTION 46

What are Operator Profiles used for?

A. To allot ClearPass roles to guest users.
B. To enforce role based access control for ClearPass Guest operator users.
C. To enforce role based access control for ClearPass Policy Manager admin users.
D. To map AD features to admin privilege levels in ClearPass Guest.
E. To enforce role based access control for Aruba Controllers.

QUESTION 47

Refer to the screenshot below:

Based on the Translation Rule configuration presented above, which of the given statements is accurate?

A. A user from group MatchAdmin will be allotted the operator profile of IT Administrators.
B. All active directory users will be allotted the operator profile of IT Administrators.
C. All admin users will be allotted the operator profile of IT Administrators.
D. A user from group Administrators will be allotted the operator profile of IT Administrators.
E. This translation rule is not valid for Active Directory administrators.

QUESTION 48

Which of the given steps are needed to use ClearPass as a TACACS+ Verification server for a network device? (Select 2)
A. Configure the ClearPass Policy Manager as an Verification server on the network device.
B. Configure ClearPass roles on the network device.
C. Configure RADIUS Enforcement Profile for the desired privilege level.
D. Configure TACACS Enforcement Profile for the desired privilege level.
E. Enable RADIUS accounting on the NAD device.

QUESTION 49

Which of the given is INACCURATE?

A. Active Directory can be used as the verification source to process TACACS+ verification requests coming to Clearpass from NAD devices
B. Active Directory can be used as the verification source to process Clearpass Guest Admin Access
C. TACACS+ verification requests got by Clearpass are always forwarded to a Windows Server that can handle these requests
D. TACACS+ verification requests from NAD devices to Clearpass are processed by a TACACS+ service
E. The local user repository in Clearpass can be used as the verification source for TACACS+ services

QUESTION 50

Which of the given is NOT a role of ClearPass Onboard?

A. Configure network settings
B. Provision device credentials
C. Remote wipe & control
D. Revoke device credentials
E. Provisioning of VPN Settings

QUESTION 51

Which of the given devices support Apple over-the-air provisioning? (Select 2)

A. Laptop running Mac OS X 10.6
B. Laptop running Mac OS X 10.8
C. iOS 5
D. Android 2.2
E. Windows XP

QUESTION 52

Refer to the screenshot below:

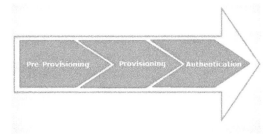

At which stage of the onboard process is workspace installed?

A. Pre-provisioning stage
B. Provisioning stage
C. Verification stage
D. After verification stage

QUESTION 53

Refer to the screenshot below:

Based on the above configuration, which of the given statements is accurate?

A. ClearPass is organized as a Root CA.
B. ClearPass is organized as the Intermediate CA.
C. ClearPass has an expired server certificate.
D. The arubatraining-REMOTELABSERVER-CA will issue user certificates for the duration of Onboarding.
E. This is not a valid trust chain since the arubatraining-REMOTELABSERVER-CA has a self-signed certificate.

QUESTION 54

What is the certificate format PKCS #7, or .p7b, used for?

A. Certificate chain
B. Certificate Signing Request
C. Certificate with an encrypted private key
D. Binary encoded X.509 certificate
E. Binary encoded X.509 certificate with public key

QUESTION 55

Refer to the screenshot below:

This verification method is operated to a service processing EAP-TLS verifications. Which of the given is INACCURATE?

A. Devices with revoked certificates will not be permitted access

B. Devices with deleted certificates will not be permitted access

C. Devices will perform OCSP check to their laptop's localhost OCSP server

D. Devices will perform OCSP check with Clearpass

QUESTION 56

Refer to the screenshot below:

Which of the given statements is correct regarding the above configuration for the private key? (Select 2)

A. The private key is stored in the user device.
B. The private key is stored in the ClearPass server.
C. More bits in the private key will reduce security, hence smallest private key size is used.

D. More bits in the private key will increase the processing time, hence smallest private key size is used.
E. The private key for TLS user certificates is not made.

QUESTION 57

Refer to the screenshot below:

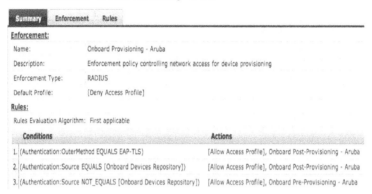

Configuration » Enforcement » Policies » Edit - Onboard Provisioning - Aruba

Enforcement Policies - Onboard Provisioning - Aruba

Summary Enforcement Rules

Enforcement:

Name:	Onboard Provisioning - Aruba
Description:	Enforcement policy controlling network access for device provisioning
Enforcement Type:	RADIUS
Default Profile:	[Deny Access Profile]

Rules:

Rules Evaluation Algorithm: First applicable

Conditions	Actions
1. (Authentication:OuterMethod EQUALS EAP-TLS)	[Allow Access Profile], Onboard Post-Provisioning - Aruba
2. (Authentication:Source EQUALS [Onboard Devices Repository])	[Allow Access Profile], Onboard Post-Provisioning - Aruba
3. (Authentication:Source NOT_EQUALS [Onboard Devices Repository])	[Allow Access Profile], Onboard Pre-Provisioning - Aruba

A worker connects a corporate laptop to the network and verifies for the first time using EAP-TLS. Based on the above Enforcement Policy configuration, what Enforcement Profile will be sent in this scenario?

A. Deny Access Profile

B. Onboard Post-Provisioning - Aruba

C. Onboard Pre-Provisioning – Aruba

D. Cannot be concluded

E. Onboard Device Repository

QUESTION 58

An Android device goes through the single-ssid onboarding process and effectively connects using EAP-TLS to the secure network. What is the order in which services are activated?

A. Onboard Provisioning, Onboard Authorization

B. Onboard Provisioning, Onboard Authorization, Onboard Provisioning

C. Onboard Authorization, Onboard Provisioning

D. Onboard Authorization, Onboard Provisioning, Onboard Authorization

E. Onboard Provisioning

QUESTION 59

Which of the given is ACCURATE of dual-SSID onboarding?

A. The device connects to the secure SSID for provisioning
B. The Onboard Authorization service is activated when the user connects to the secure SSID
C. The Onboard Provisioning service is activated when the user connects to the Provisioning SSID
D. The Onboard Authorization service is activated for the duration of the Onboarding process
E. The Onboard Authorization service is never activated

QUESTION 60

Refer to the screenshot below:

Which of the given statements is correct regarding the above configuration for 'maximum devices'?

A. It restricts the total number of On boarded devices connected to the network.
B. It restricts the total number of devices that can be provisioned by ClearPass.
C. It restricts the number of devices that a single user can Onboard.
D. It restricts the number of devices that a single user can connect to the network.
E. With this setting, the user cannot Onboard any devices.

QUESTION 61

Which of the given device kinds support Exchange ActiveSync configuration with Onboard?

A. Windows laptop
B. Apple iOS device
C. Android device
D. Mac OS X device
E. Linux Laptop

QUESTION 62

Which of the given verification protocols can be used for authenticating Windows users that are Onboarded? (Select 2)

A. PEAP with MSCHAPv2
B. EAP-GTC
C. EAP-TLS
D. PAP
E. CHAP

QUESTION 63

Refer to the screenshot. The given is seen in the Licensing tab of the Publisher after a cluster has been formed among a publisher (192.168.0.53) and subscriber (192.168.0.54):

Administration » Server Manager » Licensing

Licensing

License Summary	Servers	Applications

Cluster License Summary

	License Type	Total Count	Used Count
1	Policy Manager	1000	0
2	ClearPass Enterprise	550	0

Note: The ClearPass Enterprise license count is

Server License Summary

	Server	License Type	Total Count	Used Count
1	192.168.0.53	Policy Manager	500	0
2	192.168.0.53	ClearPass Enterprise	525	0
3	192.168.0.54	Policy Manager	500	0
4	192.168.0.54	ClearPass Enterprise	25	0

What is the maximum number of users that can be Onboarded on the

subscriber node? A. 1000
B. 550
C. 25
D. 525
E. 500

QUESTION 64

A guest self-registered through a Publisher's Register page. Which of the given will happen?

A. The guest's account will be stored in the Publisher's guest user repository, but not the Subscriber's.
B. The guest's account will be stored in both the Publisher's guest user repository and the Subscriber's guest user repository.
C. The guest's account will be stored in the Publisher's local user repository and the Subscriber's guest user repository.
D. The guest's account will be stored in the Publisher's guest user repository and the Subscriber's Onboard user repository.
E. The guest's account will JUST ONLY be stored in the Publisher's guest user repository.

QUESTION 65

Below is a network topology exhibit:

How many clusters are needed for this deployment?

A. 1
B. 3
C. 4
D. 8
E. 2

QUESTION 66

A Publisher node in a cluster goes down and Subscribers are no longer able to reach the publisher. Which of the given is accurate? (Select 2).

A. Users authenticating with the Publisher node continue to verify.
B. Users authenticating with the Subscriber nodes are no longer able to verify.
C. Users authenticating with the Publisher node are no longer able to verify.
D. Users authenticating with the Subscriber nodes continue to verify.
E. No users can verify to either the Publisher or Subscriber nodes.

QUESTION 67

Which of the given statements is accurate about the Clearpass hardware appliances?

A. DHCP can be used to allot IP addresses to management and data ports.
B. Both Management and Data Ports needs to be organized.
C. Clearpass has a default management IP of 172.16.0.254.
D. Just only static IP addresses are permitted on the management and data ports.
E. The maximum number of devices supported is 5000.

QUESTION 68

UDP Port 3799 is used for RADIUS CoA (RFC 3576). This port has been blocked by a firewall among a NAD device and ClearPass. Which of the given is accurate?

A. RADIUS Verifications will fail since the NAD won't be able to reach the ClearPass server.
B. RADIUS Verifications will not happen since the NAD won't be able to reach the ClearPass server.
C. RADIUS Verification will succeed, but Post-Verification Disconnect-Requests from ClearPass to the Controller will not be delivered.
D. RADIUS Verification will succeed, but RADIUS Access-Accept messages from ClearPass to the Controller for Change of Role will not be delivered.
E. For the duration of RADIUS verification, certificate exchange among the NAD and Clearpass will fail.

QUESTION 69

What is the aim of the Serial Port in the ClearPass appliance?

A. To connect 2 ClearPass servers together in a cluster.
B. To connect a ClearPass server to a Network Access Device.
C. For administrators to configure the ClearPass appliance using the command line.
D. For administrators to configure the ClearPass appliance using the WebUI.
E. For administrators to access Clearpass using SSH.

QUESTION 70

Presented here is a AAA profile in the Aruba Controller.

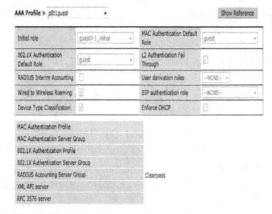

According to the configuration presented here, what would we expect to see in the ClearPass Policy Manager?

A. RADIUS accounting start-stop messages
B. RADIUS interim accounting messages
C. RADIUS interim & start-stop messages
D. No accounting messages will be seen
E. RADIUS accounting messages will be sent from the User to the Controller

QUESTION 71

Presented here is an Aruba Instant configuration screenshot

What is the aim of enabling the 'Dynamic RADIUS proxy' feature?

A. The Instant AP will proxy all RADIUS Access-Requests sent to it from users and will forward these to ClearPass.

B. The Instant AP will send a RADIUS Access-Reject packet to other Instant APs in the cluster if credentials are incorrect, to reduce the number of RADIUS requests sent to ClearPass.

C. All Instant APs in the cluster will use the Virtual Controller IP as the Source IP for RADIUS requests.

D. All Instant APs in the cluster will use the Virtual Controller IP as the Destination IP for RADIUS requests.

E. The Instant AP will proxy all RADIUS Access-Requests sent to it from Clearpass and will forward these to the users.

QUESTION 72

Refer to the screenshot below

Summary	Policy	Mapping Rules		

Policy:

Policy Name:	WLAN role mapping
Description:	
Default Role:	[Guest]

Mapping Rules:

Rules Evaluation Algorithm: First applicable

Conditions	Role Name
1. (Authorization:remotelab AD:Department EQUALS Product Management) OR (Authorization:remotelab AD:UserDN EQUALS Executive)	Executive
2. (Authorization:[Endpoints Repository]:OS Family EQUALS_IGNORE_CASE Windows)	Vendor
3. (Authorization:[Endpoints Repository]:Category CONTAINS SmartDevice) AND (Authorization:[Endpoints Repository]:OS Family EQUALS_IGNORE_CASE Apple)	iOS Device
4. (Authorization:remotelab AD:UserDN EXISTS)	[Employee]
5. (Authorization:remotelab AD:Department EQUALS HR) OR (Connection:NAD-IP-Address BELONGS_TO_GROUP HQ) OR (Date:Day-of-Week NOT_BELONGS_TO Saturday, Sunday)	HR Local
6. (Host:OSType CONTAINS Fedora) OR (Host:OSType CONTAINS Redhat) OR (Host:OSType CONTAINS Ubuntu)	Linux User
7. (Connection:NAD-IP-Address BELONGS_TO_GROUP Remote NAD)	Remote Employee

If a user from the unit "HR" connects on Monday using their Windows Laptop to a switch that belongs to the Device Group HQ, what role is allotted to the user in Clearpass?

A. Executive
B. HR Local
C. Worker
D. Guest
E. Vendor

QUESTION 73

Refer to the screenshot below

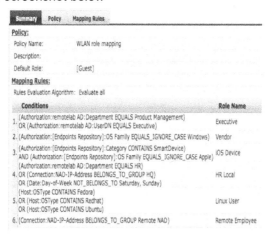

If a user from the unit "HR" connects on Monday to a switch that belongs to the Device Group Remote NAD, what roles are allotted to the user in Clearpass? (Select 2)

A. Executive
B. Remote Worker
C. iOS Device
D. Guest
E. HR Local

QUESTION 74

Refer to the screenshot below

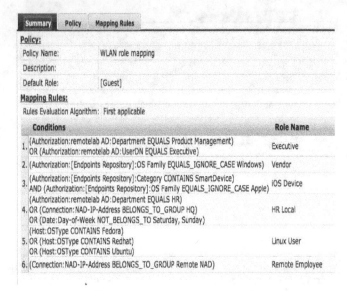

| Summary | Policy | Mapping Rules |

Policy:

Policy Name:	WLAN role mapping
Description:	
Default Role:	[Guest]

Mapping Rules:

Rules Evaluation Algorithm: First applicable

Conditions	Role Name
1. (Authorization:remotelab AD:Department EQUALS Product Management) OR (Authorization:remotelab AD:UserDN EQUALS Executive)	Executive
2. (Authorization:[Endpoints Repository]:OS Family EQUALS_IGNORE_CASE Windows)	Vendor
3. (Authorization:[Endpoints Repository]:Category CONTAINS SmartDevice) AND (Authorization:[Endpoints Repository]:OS Family EQUALS_IGNORE_CASE Apple)	iOS Device
4. (Authorization:remotelab AD:Department EQUALS HR) OR (Connection:NAD-IP-Address BELONGS_TO_GROUP HQ) OR (Date:Day-of-Week NOT_BELONGS_TO Saturday, Sunday)	HR Local
5. (Host:OSType CONTAINS Fedora) OR (Host:OSType CONTAINS Redhat) OR (Host:OSType CONTAINS Ubuntu)	Linux User
6. (Connection:NAD-IP-Address BELONGS_TO_GROUP Remote NAD)	Remote Employee

If a user from the unit "QA" verifies from a laptop running MAC OS X, what role is allotted to the user in Clearpass?

A. iOS Device

B. Remote Worker

C. HR Local

D. Guest

E. Executive

QUESTION 75

Which of the given statements is NOT accurate about the configuration of Active Directory (AD) as an External Verification Server in Clearpass?

A. Clearpass must join the AD domain when PEAP and MSCHAPv2 are used as the verification kind.

B. The bind DN for an AD can be in the administrator@domain format.

C. Clearpass cannot be a member of more than one AD domain.

D. The list of features fetched from the AD can be customized.

E. Clearpass nodes in a cluster can join different AD domains.

QUESTION 76

Which of the given statements is NOT accurate about the configuration of a generic LDAP server as an External Verification Server in Clearpass?

A. The bind DN can be in the administrator@domain format.
B. The list of features fetched from an LDAP server can be customized.
C. An LDAP Browser can be used to search the Base DN.
D. Multiple LDAP servers cannot be organized as verification sources.
E. Generic LDAP servers can be used as verification sources.

QUESTION 77

Refer to the screenshot below:

Configuration » Authentication » Sources » Add - remotelab AD

Authentication Sources - remotelab AD

Summary	General	Primary	**Attributes**

Specify filter queries used to fetch authentication and authorization attributes

Filter Name	Attribute Name	Alias Name	Enabled As
1. Authentication	dn	UserDN	-
	department	Department	Role, Attribute
	title	Title	Attribute
	company	company	-
	memberOf	memberOf	Role, Attribute
	telephoneNumber	Phone	Attribute
	mail	Email	Attribute

Based on the Attribute configuration presented above, which of the given statements is accurate?

A. Just only the attribute values of unit and memberOf can be used in role mapping policies.
B. Just only the attribute values of title, telephoneNumber, mail can be used in role mapping policies.
C. Just only the attribute values of corporation can be used in role mapping policies.
D. The attribute values of unit and memberOf are directly operated as ClearPass roles.
E. The attribute values of unit, title, memberOf, telephoneNumber, mail are directly operated as ClearPass roles.

QUESTION 78

How is Authorization used in a Policy Service? Refer to the exhibit below:

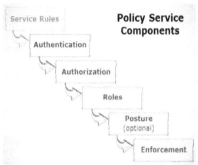

A. It lets us to use features stored in databases in role mapping and Enforcement.
B. It lets us to use features stored in databases in role mapping just only, but not Enforcement.
C. It lets us to use features stored in databases in Enforcement just only, but not role mapping.
D. It lets us to use features stored in external databases for Enforcement, but authorization does not use internal databases for reference.
E. It lets us to use features stored in internal databases for Enforcement, but authorization does not use external databases for reference.

QUESTION 79

Refer to the given Service configuration:

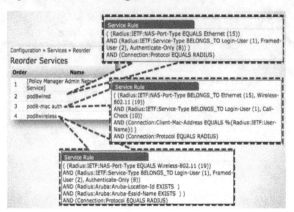

A user connects for the first time to an Aruba access point wireless SSID named "pod8wireless-guest-SSID". The SSID has web login verification with RADIUS MAC verification allowed and ClearPass is the verification server. The user hasn't yet launched their web browser. Which service will be activated?

A. pod8wired

B. pod8-mac auth

C. pod8wireless

D. [Policy Manager Admin Network Service]

E. No service will be activated

QUESTION 80

Refer to the given configuration for a VLAN Enforcement Policy:

Based on the Policy configuration, if an Engineer connects to the network on Saturday using WEBAUTH verification, what VLAN will be allotted?

A. Full Access VLAN
B. Worker Vlan
C. Deny Access
D. Internet VLAN
E. There is not enough data to conclude the VLAN result.

QUESTION 81

Refer to the given configuration for a VLAN Enforcement Policy:

Based on the Policy configuration, if an Engineer connects to the network on Saturday using RADIUS verification, what VLAN will be allotted?

A. Full Access VLAN
B. Worker Vlan
C. Deny Access
D. Internet VLAN
E. There is not enough data to conclude the VLAN result.

QUESTION 82

Refer to the given configuration for a VLAN Enforcement Policy:
Based on the profile configuration, which of the given VLANs will be allotted to the user when this profile is used?

A. VLAN 13
B. VLAN 6
C. VLAN 10
D. VLAN 1
E. VLAN 10800

QUESTION 83

Refer to the given configuration for a VLAN Enforcement Policy:

Which of the given statements is accurate for the above configuration?

A. This profile will be operated to requests coming from an end user in the Device Group HQ.
B. This profile will be operated to requests coming from a Network Access Device in the Device Group HQ.
C. The profile will be operated to requests processed by a ClearPass appliance in Device Group HQ.
D. This profile will be operated to all users.
E. This profile will be operated to RADIUS requests that have timed out after 10800 seconds.

QUESTION 84

Which of the given checks are made with OnGuard posture evaluation in Clearpass? (Select 3)

A. Peer-to-peer application checks
B. User role check
C. EAP TLS certificate validity
D. Registry keys
E. Operating System version

QUESTION 85

Refer to the screenshot below:

Based on the above Enforcement Profile configuration, which of the given statements is correct?

A. The Enforcement Profile sends an unhealthy role value to the Network Access Device.
B. The Enforcement Profile sends a limited access vlan value to the Network Access Device.
C. The Enforcement Profile sends a message to the OnGuard Agent on the user device.
D. The Enforcement Profile sends a message to the OnGuard Agent on the Controller.
E. A RADIUS CoA message is sent to bounce the user.

ANSWER

1. Correct Answer: BC
2. Correct Answer: B
3. Correct Answer: C
4. Correct Answer: B
5. Correct Answer: ACE
6. Correct Answer: D
7. Correct Answer: A
8. Correct Answer: B
9. Correct Answer: D
10. Correct Answer: AC
11. Correct Answer: E
12. Correct Answer: BD
13. Correct Answer: D
14. Correct Answer: A
15. Correct Answer: C
16. Correct Answer: B
17. Correct Answer: AC
18. Correct Answer: C
19. Correct Answer: AC
20. Correct Answer: D
21. Correct Answer: C
22. Correct Answer: C
23. Correct Answer: D
24. Correct Answer: C
25. Correct Answer: D
26. Correct Answer: ACD
27. Correct Answer: AD
28. Correct Answer: D
29. Correct Answer: AD
30. Correct Answer: B
31. Correct Answer: B
32. Correct Answer: A
33. Correct Answer: C
34. Correct Answer: B
35. Correct Answer: C
36. Correct Answer: AD
37. Correct Answer: A
38. Correct Answer: B
39. Correct Answer: B
40. Correct Answer: B

41. Correct Answer: C
42. Correct Answer: D
43. Correct Answer: A
44. Correct Answer: A
45. Correct Answer: E
46. Correct Answer: B
47. Correct Answer: D
48. Correct Answer: AD
49. Correct Answer: C
50. Correct Answer: C
51. Correct Answer: BC
52. Correct Answer: D
53. Correct Answer: B
54. Correct Answer: A
55. Correct Answer: C
56. Correct Answer: AD
57. Correct Answer: B
58. Correct Answer: B
59. Correct Answer: D
60. Correct Answer: C
61. Correct Answer: B
62. Correct Answer: AC
63. Correct Answer: B
64. Correct Answer: B
65. Correct Answer: C
66. Correct Answer: CD
67. Correct Answer: D
68. Correct Answer: C
69. Correct Answer: C
70. Correct Answer: A
71. Correct Answer: C
72. Correct Answer: E
73. Correct Answer: BE
74. Correct Answer: D
75. Correct Answer: C
76. Correct Answer: A
77. Correct Answer: D
78. Correct Answer: A
79. Correct Answer: B
80. Correct Answer: B
81. Correct Answer: D
82. Correct Answer: C
83. Correct Answer: B
84. Correct Answer: ADE

85. Correct Answer: C

www.ingramcontent.com/pod-product-compliance
Lightning Source LLC
LaVergne TN
LVHW051613050326
832903LV00033B/4485